WEIRD MONUMENTS
of CANADA

Quirky and Ridiculously
Oversized Roadside Attractions

WEIRD MONUMENTS
of CANADA

Quirky and Ridiculously
Oversized Roadside Attractions

Nicholle Carrière

BLUE
BIKE
BOOKS

Introduction

Canada is a huge country, no question! So how do small communities get noticed and attract tourists? Well, they build something big, of course!

Canadians have a love affair with gigantic roadside attractions or, as I have dubbed them, monuments. They are often kind of quirky and a little cartoony, but they are *always* enormous. They may feature a town's mascot, advertise something that a community is famous for or commemorate an event or historical figure. Sometimes, like Watson Lake's Signpost Forest, they begin accidentally. The young, homesick soldier who put up the first signpost pointing to his hometown in 1942 had no idea he had started a trend that would snowball into a crazy conglomeration of more than 100,000 signs.

This collection of weird monuments features something from every province and territory. Some are funny and informal, whereas others are more serious and artistic. They can be found in provincial capitals, as well as in tiny communities. All are huge, and most are bigger than life.

Many are billed as the "world's largest," although that claim to fame may be disputed and can change over time. There seems to be an element of competition in creating these monuments. Whenever a town decides to build one, research is conducted into existing monuments, and the new statue is then built to be just a little bit larger.

Finally, this book would not have been possible without the generous spirit of photographers who allow their works to be used in publications such as this. I would also like to thank the administrators in towns and villages who responded enthusiastically to my queries for photos—especially those who answered with something like, "Wait a minute, I'll just go outside and take a picture for you!"

The weird monuments depicted here are only a small sampling of the hundreds that can be found all across our country. They are unique, interesting and worth seeing for yourself. Sounds like a good reason for a road trip!

Sea Creatures
Victoria

Year built: c1954
Refurbished in 2013–14
Material: concrete
Location: Cadboro-Gyro Park

The playground in this popular park features giant statues of an octopus, a salmon and Caddy the Cadborosaurus. A sea serpent that supposedly inhabits the bay, Caddy was named by newspaper editor Archie Willis after a reported sighting of the creature in 1933.

World's Tallest Tin Soldier
New Westminster

Year built: 2000
Size: 9.8 m high
Weight: 4.5 t
Material: stainless steel
Location: New Westminster Quay Public Market

The giant gendarme is modelled on a sergeant major of the Royal Engineers, who founded New Westminster in 1859. The statue was built by the Sheet Metal Workers International Association and the BC Sheet Metal Association. A plaque states that the boots are size 60 E27. The metal man contains a time capsule that will be opened in 2025.

House Sparrows
Vancouver

Year built: 2010
Size: 5.5 m high
Weight: 1900 kg
Material: expanded polystyrene foam (EPS) on a steel armature with polyurea skin; cast bronze legs
Location: Southeast False Creek Olympic Plaza in the Olympic Village

Myfanwy MacLeod's *The Birds*, a pair of larger-than-life house sparrows was created as part of Vancouver's Olympic and Paralympic Public Art Program. The work is intended to bring attention to the dangers of introducing non-native species into an ecosystem.

World's Largest Ice Hockey Stick and Puck
Duncan

The giant stick and puck were commissioned by the BC government for Expo '86. After the event, a Canada-wide contest was held to determine the attraction's final home. The community of Duncan raised $150,000 in cash and donated goods and services to win the competition and the oversize sports equipment.

Year built: 1988
Size: 62.5 m long
Weight: 28 t
Material: steel-reinforced Douglas-fir beams
Location: Cowichan Community Centre

Mr. PG
Prince George

Year built: 1983, to replace the original wooden statue built in 1960
Size: 8.2 m high; head 1.5 m in diameter
Material: fibreglass and sheet metal painted to look like wood
Location: Highway 16, next to the Prince George Playhouse

Mr. PG symbolizes the importance of the forestry industry to the city of Prince George. He had a time capsule in his chest that was removed when the statue was refurbished in 2012.

Terex Titan
Sparwood

This giant truck was once used in the Kaiser Resources coal mine. It can haul nearly 320 tonnes, and the box is capable of holding two Greyhound buses and two pickup trucks. Each tire is 3.4 metres high and weighs 3.6 tonnes.

Year built: 1994
Size: 20.1 m long, 6.7 m high, 7.8 m wide
Weight: 236 t
Material: steel
Location: north side of Highway 3 at the Visitor Information Centre

World's Tallest Totem Pole
Alert Bay

Year built: raised in 1973
Size: 52.7 m high, in two sections (51.2 m and 1.5 m long)
Material: cedar wood
Location: next to the 'Namgis Big House

This towering totem pole, created by six 'Namgis carvers, was completed in the late 1960s but not raised until 1973. The figures on the pole include a whale, wolf, thunderbird, bear, salmon and raven, among others. They represent some of the tribes of the Kwakwaka'wakw Nation.

Coho Salmon
Sandspit

An oversize salmon sculpture entitled *Spirit of Sandspit* welcomes visitors to this small community on Moresby Island in Haida Gwaii. Sandspit, the largest settlement on the island, is a major sport-fishing and tourist destination. The sculpture was designed by local artist Lon Sharp.

Year built: 2002
Material: cedar wood and copper sheeting
Location: outside the Sandspit airport

World's Tallest Cross-country Skis
100 Mile House

Year built: 1987
Size: *Skis:* 12 m high;
Poles: 9 m high
Weight: 544 kg
Material: aluminum
Location: next to the
South Cariboo Visitor
Centre

The town of 100 Mile House calls itself the "International Nordic Ski Capital" and is one of the foremost cross-country ski vacation destinations in Canada. The super-sized skis and poles were created as a community project to celebrate the Cariboo Marathon.

Woodenhead
Revelstoke

Year built: c1940
Material: cedar wood covered with fibreglass
Location: Woodenhead Park, just off the Trans-Canada Highway

Peter Fuoco, head timekeeper on the construction crew building the Big Bend Highway in the 1930s, sculpted a large cedar tree stump into a human head. The sculpture was set beside the highway, where it became one of BC's first road safety warnings. It featured a sign that read: "Don't Be Wooden Headed. Drive Carefully. You'll live to enjoy the scenery more and longer." After the Roger's Pass section of the Trans-Canada Highway was completed, the head was moved to Revelstoke. In 2005, Woodenhead was coated in fibreglass and painted, and placed under a protective roof.

Ogopogo
Kelowna

Size: 1.6 m high, 7.9 m long
Material: fibreglass
Location: City Park near Okanagan Lake

The Interior Salish people named the creature in Okanagan Lake *N'ha-a-itk,* "lake demon," and sightings date back to the 19th century. The name *Ogopogo* comes from a 1924 music hall song called "The Ogo-Pogo: The Funny Fox-Trot."

Canada's Largest Freestanding Cuckoo Clock
Kimberley

Year built: 1972
Size: *Clock:* 6.7 m high, 3.7 m wide, 3.7 m deep;
Clock face: 1.8 m in diameter; *Happy Hans:* 1.2 m high
Location: Platzl pedestrian mall

In 1972, the mining town of Kimberley reinvented itself as the "Bavarian Town of the Rockies" (even though it's actually in the Purcell Range) to attract tourists. Happy Hans, the town's mascot, pops out every hour to yodel. If you can't wait, insert a loonie into the clock, and Hans will emerge.

Water Wheel
Fort Steele

Year built: moved to Fort Steele in 1965
Size: 9.8 m in diameter, 2.1 m wide
Material: wood
Location: Fort Steele Heritage Town

The giant water wheel was built in 1934 for the Perry Creek Gold Mine, 25 kilometres west of Fort Steele. It powered two electric generators that pumped 600 gallons (2270 litres) of water per minute from the mine. The wheel turned at a rate of 6.9 revolutions per minute on a shaft that was 15 centimetres in diameter.

Wheelchair
Williams Lake

Location: at the intersection of Highways 97 and 20

Lets continue to **Work Together**, and make Williams Lake "100% Wheelchair Accessible". And one day this chair will be in a museum! Thank You, Williams Lake for Helping Rick Hansens Dream become a Reality.

The wheelchair commemorates Canadian Paralympic champion Rick Hansen's dedication to spinal cord research, as well as the Wheels in Motion committee of Williams Lake. Rick Hansen is a Williams Lake native, and Wheels in Motion is now part of the Rick Hansen Institute.

Talus Balls
Edmonton, AB

Year built: 2012
Size: nearly 1000 balls of various diameters
Material: stainless steel
Location: next to the Whitemud Freeway on the east side of the Quesnell Bridge

More than just a pile of shiny balls, this sculpture is designed to reflect the changing colours of the landscape through the seasons of the year. Talus is a geological term for an accumulation of gravel, and Los Angeles artists Benjamin Ball and Gaston Nogues intended their work to suggest a pile of rocks that you might see along the North Saskatchewan River.

World's Largest Dragonfly
Wabamun, AB

The giant insect was designed and built by structural welder Frank Phaneuf. For added realism, a local artist airbrushed the dragonfly. The Wabamun statue displaces the giant dragonfly in Ottertail, Minnesota, as the world's largest of its kind.

Year built: 2009
Size: *Dragonfly:* nearly 10 m long; *Pole:* 6 m high
Material: propane tanks, airplane wings and a light pole
Location: at the entrance to the town

Twelve Foot Davis
Peace River, AB

Year built: 1961
Size: 3.7 m
Weight: 900 kg
Material: laminated cedar
Location: River Front Park

Henry Fuller Davis (c1818–1900) was a prospector and trader. He got his nickname because he mined $15,000 worth of gold from a plot that was only 12 feet (3.6 metres) wide. The statue was carved by Kaj Neilsen of Victoria, BC.

World's Largest Beaver
Beaverlodge, AB

Year built: 2004
Size: *Beaver:* 4.6 m high, 5.5 m long, 3 m wide; *Log:* 6.1 m long, 1.5 m in diameter
Weight: *Beaver:* 680 kg; *Log:* 680 kg
Material: EPS foam on a metal frame; coated with polyurea
Location: on Highway 43 next to the Beaverlodge Cultural Centre

Beaverlodge built its gargantuan beaver as a town landmark to celebrate its 75th anniversary. The project was the brainchild of local entrepreneur Alex Lojczyc, who thought it would attract visitors to the community.

World's Largest Ukrainian Sausage
Mundare, AB

Year built: 2001
Size: 12.8 m
Weight: 5.4 t
Material: fibreglass
Location: Sawchuk Street and 50th Avenue

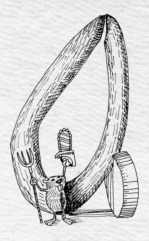

The giant kielbasa was created as a tribute to Stawnichy's Meat Processing, a local company founded in 1959. Stawnichy's has made the town of Mundare synonymous with Ukrainian sausage, and although the company produces over 80 meat and Ukrainian food products, its specialty remains kielbasa.

World's Largest Easter Egg (Pysanka)
Vegreville, AB

Year built: 1974
Size: 9.4 m high,
7.8 m long, 5.5 m
wide
Weight: *Egg:* 2.3 t;
Base: 12.2 t
Material: aluminum
Location: Elk's Park
on the north side of
Highway 16A

This extraordinary egg was built to commemorate the 100th
Anniversary of the Royal Canadian Mounted Police. It turns in
the wind like a weathervane. The gold, silver and bronze colours
represent prosperity.

UFO Landing Pad
St. Paul, AB

Year built: 1967
Size: 12 m in diameter
Weight: 118 t
Material: steel-reinforced concrete
Location: next to the tourist information centre

The UFO Landing Pad was built to be both a tourist attraction and to celebrate Canada's centennial. A UFO exhibit in the adjacent tourist information centre features photographs of UFOs, crop circles and reports of UFO sightings and encounters of all kinds.

World's Largest Oil Lamp
Donalda, AB

Year built: 2000
Size: 12.8 m high, 5.2 m wide at the base
Material: *Base:* sheet metal; *Globe:* fibreglass
Location: at the east end of Main Street

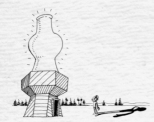

The giant lamp was created as a millennium project by the village, the Donalda Museum and the local Agricultural Society. Every night at dusk, a 400-watt street lamp illuminates the structure from the inside. The museum across the street houses the world's largest collection of oil lamps, with over 1000 lamps, as well as many local artifacts.

World's Largest Dinosaur
Drumheller, AB

Year built: 2000
Size: 25 m tall, 46 m long
Weight: 65.7 t
Material: fibreglass and steel
Location: Drumheller Visitor Information Center

This larger-than-life T-Rex is one of the feature attractions in the "Dinosaur Capital of the World." A flight of 62 steps climbs through the inside of the statue and onto a viewing platform in its mouth. The monument is about four times larger than an actual T-Rex.

Pinto MacBean
Bow Island, AB

Year built: 1992
Size: 5.5 m high
Material: fibreglass
Location: beside the Visitor Centre on Highway 3

Bow Island, a small town in southeastern Alberta, is the "Bean Capital of the West." The town mascot, Pinto MacBean, was created to symbolize the important role that the dry edible bean industry plays in the area and to attract tourists to the town.

Starship USS Enterprise
Vulcan, AB

Year built: 1995
Size: *Ship:* 9.4 m long, 2.7 m wide; *Base:* 2.7 m high, 5.8 m long
Weight: 5.1 t
Material: steel on a concrete base
Location: at the Vulcan Tourism and Trek Station on the west side of Highway 23

Vulcan decided to capitalize on its name and created a *Star Trek*–related attraction to bring tourists to the community. Besides providing information, the station has a display of *Star Trek* memorabilia and provides unique photo opportunities and activities. The ship's pedestal includes text in alien languages such as Klingon.

Mushrooms
Vilna, AB

Settled in 1907 mostly by Central European immigrants, Vilna is known as the "Mushroom Capital of the World." The mushrooms are the species *Tricholoma ustale,* known as the burnt knight. Mushroom hunting is popular in the area, and this particular mushroom is abundant. It is a traditional ingredient in ethnic dishes of the region.

Year built: 1993
Size: 6.1 m tall (tallest mushroom); *Heads:* 3 m, 3.7 m and 4.6 m in diameter; *Stem:* 46 cm in diameter
Material: steel
Location: in Mushroom Park, one block east of Main Street

Border Markers
Lloydminster, AB and SK

Year built: 1994, replaced in 2003
Size: 30.5 m high
Material: steel
Location: from City Hall to the intersection of Highways 16 and 17

Lloydminster is the only Canadian city that straddles two provinces. To mark the border, which is the 4th Meridian, four large, red pillars resembling survey markers were erected. The narrow gap that runs down the centre of each tower marks the actual border. Each marker also represents one of four themes: Oil and Gas, the Barr Colonists, Agriculture and First Nations and Métis.

Quilly Willy
Porcupine Plain, SK

Year built: 1986
Size: 4 m high
Material: fibreglass over a welded steel frame, wooden base
Location: Keyowski Roadside Park

Quilly Willy, the "World's Largest Porcupine" and beloved town mascot, embodies the friendliness of this rural community. Designer Hugh Vassos also designed the bison monument in Melville. Quilly Willy's flag changes from time to time to reflect local events.

Coffeepot and Cup
Davidson, SK

Year built: 1996
Size: 7.3 m high
Material: sheet metal
Location: at the junction
of Highways 11 and 44

This agricultural community is known as the "midway town" because its central location between Saskatoon, Regina and Moose Jaw makes it a meeting place for business people and organizations. The giant monument represents the town's reputation for hospitality and friendliness. The massive coffeepot could hold 150,000 cups of coffee.

Mountie and Horse
North Battleford, SK

Year built: 1966
Size: 7 m high
(to top of lance)
Weight: 544 kg
Material: fibreglass
over a welded steel
frame
Location: next
to the tourist
information centre
at the intersection of
Highways 16 and 40

The statue was unveiled in 1966 in celebration of the
city's golden jubilee and the upcoming Canadian centennial.
It was originally part of the heritage village on the Western
Development Museum grounds.

Giant Hockey Cards
Kelvington, SK

Year built: 1992
Size: 3.7 m high, 7.3 m long; *Each Card:* 2.4 m high, 1.2 m wide
Material: Duraboard
Location: on the west side of Highway 38 next to the golf course

The enormous cards feature NHL hockey stars from the Kelvington area: Lloyd Gronsdahl, Barry Melrose, Joe Kocur, Wendel Clark, Kerry Clark and Kory Kocur. The cards also include each player's stats. The monument was designed by Edd Feairs and the portraits painted by local artist Rose Steadman.

Ox and Cart
Paradise Hill, SK

The ox and cart were built to commemorate the Carlton Trail, which passed over the location where the monument stands. The trail was the overland route that connected Fort Edmonton with Fort Garry (Winnipeg), a distance of almost 2000 kilometres. Oxen pulling Red River carts would have been a common sight on the trail.

Year built: 1993
Size: *Ox*: 3 m high, weight 454 kg; *Cart*: 3 m high
Material: fibreglass (ox and cart wheels), metal (reins) and wood (cart)
Location: on the southwest corner of Highway 3 and 1st Avenue (town access road)

Red-headed Woodpecker Welcome Sign
Leader, SK

Year built: 2004
Size: 4.9 m high, 3.0 m wide
Material: fibreglass
Location: entrance to town

This is one of many bigger-than-life statues of local wildlife created by the late Ralph Berg and Grant McLaughlin. In various locations throughout the town, you can find a group of burrowing owls; a mule deer; a western meadowlark, prairie rattlesnake and prickly pear cactus; a long-billed curlew and loggerhead shrike; a ferruginous hawk with nest and chicks; a crouching bobcat; a lake sturgeon; and a pair of Ord's kangaroo rats.

Wheat Stalk
Sceptre, SK

Year built: 1990
Size: 10 m tall
Material: steel
Location: at the corner of Railway Street and Kingsway (Main) Street

The village of Sceptre, population 99, has a number of public art works, including fire hydrants painted as cartoon characters, murals and the tallest wheat plant in North America. The community is also home to the Great Sand Hills Interpretive Centre.

Mac the Moose
Moose Jaw, SK

Year built: 1984; moved to present location in 2004
Size: 9.8 m high
Weight: 9 t
Material: framework of metal pipes and strips covered with metal mesh and concrete
Location: in front of the Tourism Moose Jaw Visitor Centre on the south side of Highway 1

The "World's Largest Moose," Mac is one of Canada's most photographed roadside attractions. The Moose Jaw mascot is named after late city alderman Les MacKenzie. In 2013, Mac the Moose was voted "Moose Jaw's Best Celebrity" by the *Moose Jaw Times Herald*.

Lesia the Ukrainian Girl
Canora, SK

Year built: 1980
Size: 7.6 m high
Material: fibreglass
Location: east side of Highway 9 off Barschel Avenue

Lesia was built to commemorate the 75th anniversary of the province of Saskatchewan and the town of Canora. Dressed in traditional Ukrainian garb, she holds a tray with bread and salt, traditional Eastern European gifts of welcome.

Corner Gas Set
Rouleau, SK

Year built: 2004
Location: just off
Highway 39

The town of Rouleau was the filming location for the Canadian sitcom *Corner Gas* (2004–09). After the series ended, the set was allowed to fall into disrepair. Seeing an opportunity, local entrepreneur Sylvain Senecal bought the buildings and converted them into a souvenir shop and museum.

World's Largest Red Paper Clip
Kipling, SK

The village of Kipling shot to fame after an unlikely sequence of trades, which began with a red paper clip, earned Montréaler Kyle Macdonald a house in the community. The house is now often referred to as the "Red Paper Clip House," and the village created the statue as part of the terms of the trade.

Year built: 2007
Size: 4.6 m tall, 1 m wide, 13.9 m long
Weight: 1380 kg
Material: steel
Location: Bell Park

Flinty
Flin Flon, MB

Year built: 1962, restored in 1989
Size: 7.5 m high
Material: fibreglass
Location: next to the Flin Flon Museum

The town's namesake, Josiah Flintabbatey Flonatin (aka "Flinty"), was the protagonist of the 1905 novel *The Sunless City* by J.E. Preston Muddock. When prospector Tom Creighton discovered the rich mineral vein that led to the founding of a mine and later the town, he thought of the book and christened the settlement Flin Flon. The statue was designed by cartoonist Al Capp, of *Li'l Abner* fame.

Sara the Camel
Glenboro, MB

Sara the Camel symbolizes the Spirit Sands, also known as the Manitoba Desert, located in Spruce Woods Provincial Park, about 10 kilometres north of Glenboro. The statue was created by sculptor George Barone and trucked to its location in two pieces. A project of the Glenboro and District Chamber of Commerce, Sara is used to promote the town and the Spirit Sands.

Year built: 1978, refurbished in 2008
Size: *Camel:* 5 m high
Weight: over 900 kg
Material: fibreglass and metal; concrete base
Location: in Camel Park, at the junction of Cochrane Street and Highway 2

Fire Hydrant
Elm Creek, MB

Year built: 2001
Size: *Hydrant:* 9 m high; *Wrench:* 4.5 m high; *Chain:* 3.7 m long
Location: next to the firehall on Railway Avenue at Gladys Street

The giant fire hydrant was built by the area's volunteer firefighters and unveiled on Canada Day in 2001. A real fire hydrant stands in front of the gargantuan replica.

World's Largest Curling Rock
Arborg, MB

The town of Arborg loves curling, and the history of the game in the community dates back to 1945. The giant curling rock was created to celebrate the success of two local high school curling teams that won the Provincial High School Curling Championship title in 1948, 1949 and 1988.

Year built: 2005
Size: 2.1 m tall, 4.2 m across
Weight: 1.5 t
Material: steel, foam and fibreglass on top of steel support beams
Location: just outside the Arborg Bifrost Curling Club

Viking
Gimli, MB

Year built: 1967
Size: 4.6 m tall
Material: fibreglass
Location: at the south end of Second Avenue

Gimli's massive Viking honours the town's Icelandic heritage. A centennial project sponsored by the local Chamber of Commerce, the statue was designed by Gissur Eliasson, a professor at University of Manitoba, and created by Italian Canadian sculptor George Barone. President Asgeir Asgeirson of Iceland unveiled the monument on July 30, 1967, at the Icelandic Festival.

Happy Rock
Gladstone, MB

Year built: 1993
Size: 11 m tall
Weight: 1360 kg
Material: fibreglass
Location: northeast side of Highway 16

Jerry Wickstead's design "Happy Rock," a play on the town's name ("glad stone," get it?) was selected as the winner of a 1984 contest to create a town mascot. The monument serves as the town's visitor information centre and even appeared on a postage stamp in 2010.

S-S-Sam and S-S-Sara the Gartersnakes
Inwood, MB

Year built: 1995
Size: 4.6 m high; *Sam:* 7.6 m long; *Sara:* 8.8 m long
Material: *Snakes:* rebar and polyurethane foam covered with fibreglass; *Base:* granite and limestone rocks
Location: at the intersection of Main Street and Railway Avenue

The gartersnake monument was constructed to attract tourists to the hamlet of Inwood. The area is famous for red-sided gartersnake dens, and thousands of snakes emerge every May to mate. The nearby Narcisse Snake Dens feature the world's highest concentration of red-sided gartersnakes, and scientists from around the world come yearly to study the reptiles.

Chuck the Channel Cat
Selkirk, MB

Year built: 1986
Size: 7.6 m tall
Material: fibreglass
Location: on Main Street in front of Smitty's Restaurant

Selkirk advertises itself as the "Catfish Capital of the World" and is a mecca for anglers. The name Chuck honours the late Chuck Norquay, an avid local sport fisherman who drowned while fishing in the Red River.

Bears on Broadway
Winnipeg, MB

Year built: 2005
Size: 2.1 m tall
Weight: 3600 kg
Material: concrete
Location: various locations throughout the city centre

In 2005, 62 bears were decorated by various local artists as part of the "Bears on Broadway" project. The statues were created as a fundraiser and to celebrate the 75th anniversary of CancerCare Manitoba.

Tommy the Turtle
Boissevain, MB

Year built: 1974
Size: 7 m tall,
2.7 m wide
Weight: 4.5 t
Material: fibreglass
and resin
Location: at the
corner of Mountain
Street and
Highway 10

Why a turtle for a town mascot? Boissevain is located close
to Turtle Mountain and Turtle Mountain Provincial Park. It even
held a "Turtle Derby" from 1972 to 2001. The statue was
designed and built by George Barone, who created many other
town monuments. In 2014, the town "shell-ebrated" Tommy's
40th birthday.

World's Largest Pumpkin
Roland, MB

Year built: 1990
Size: 3.7 m high,
3.7 m wide
Weight: 763 kg
Material: steel rods
covered with wire mesh
and fibreglass
Location: southwest of
town on Highway 23

The small village of Roland,
which has a population of only
300, is known for growing
really big pumpkins. The
community's monumental
squash was built to honour
local Pumpkin King Edgar
VanWyck, who made it into the
Guinness Book of World Records
in 1977 for growing the
world's largest pumpkin,
which weighed a whopping
560 kilograms.

Sunflower Painting
Altona, MB

Year built: 1997
Size: *Painting*: 9.8 m high, 7.3 m wide; *Easel:* 24.4 m tall
Weight: 13.6 t
Material: *Painting*: 24 sheets of 3/4" fir plywood and 17 gallons of paint; *Easel:* tubular steel
Location: behind the Multiplex

Known as the "Sunflower Capital of Canada," Altona is also home to the world's largest replica of the famous painting *Sunflowers,* by Vincent van Gogh. Artist Cameron Cross created the work as part of the worldwide Van Gogh Project.

Sundial Folly
Toronto, ON

Year built: 1995
Size: *Lake wall:* 25 m long; *Sphere:* 6 m in diameter; *Reflecting Pool:* 1.2 m above the lake; *Waterfall:* 1.2 m high, 3.2 m wide
Material: concrete, steel and water
Location: Harbour Square Park

Sundial Folly, by artists John Fung and Paul Figueiredo, is a gigantic piece of public art that comprises a concrete lake wall, a cast-concrete hollow sphere, a lake-fed reflecting pool, a small waterfall and a large, rust-coloured steel rectangle. The sphere is bisected by a 1.2-metre-wide opening that allows it to function as a sundial and lets people go inside.

Spider
Ottawa, ON

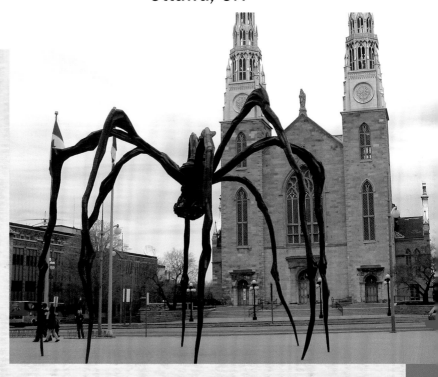

The gigantic spider sculpture, entitled *Maman*, by Franco-American artist Louise Bourgeois, was purchased by the National Gallery for $ 3.2 million. Despite its fearsome appearance, the enormous arachnid symbolizes fertility and motherhood—it carries an egg sac with 20 eggs in its underbelly.

Year built: 2004
Size: 9.25 m tall
Weight: 8165 kg
Material: *Spider:* steel and bronze; *Eggs:* white marble
Location: in front of the National Gallery

Spirit Catcher
Barrie, ON

Year built: 1986
Size: 21 m high, 25 m wide
Weight: 18 t
Material: COR-TEN steel
Location: at the base of Maple Street on the waterfront of Kempenfelt Bay

Originally created for Expo '86 in Vancouver, sculptor Ron Baird's *Spirit Catcher* was purchased by the Helen McCrea Peacock Foundation (Toronto) for $230,000 and moved to its present location in 1987. The sculpture has 16 kinetic quills, which rock back and forth when the wind blows, as well as a pair of kinetic antennae.

Miners' Memorial
Kirkland Lake, ON

Year built: 1994
Size: 10 m high
Weight: 40 t
Material: black granite with bronze figures
Location: near the Museum of Northern History at the Sir Harry Oakes Chateau

Although only a few mines remain in the area today, in the 1930s, Kirkland Lake was home to seven gold mines. The Miners' Memorial was created to honour all miners, both living and deceased. Everything on the monument is local and authentic—the stone was quarried in the area, and the mining equipment and bolts used to hold the memorial together were taken from a mine.

Canada Goose
Wawa, ON

Year built: 1963, to replace the 1960 plaster version
Size: 8.5 m high, 6.7 m long, wingspan 6.1 m
Weight: 2 t
Material: steel
Location: next to the tourist information centre at the junction of the Trans-Canada and Highway 101

When the last section of the Trans-Canada Highway opened in 1960, the road bypassed the town's centre and local businessmen felt that they had to do something to encourage visitors to go into Wawa. Why a goose? The town takes its name from the Ojibwe word *wewe*, meaning "wild goose." Sadly, the monument is in poor condition and efforts are underway to raise funds to restore it.

Big Nickel
Sudbury, ON

Sudbury's Big Nickel, the world's largest coin, is a giant-sized reproduction of a 1951 nickel, designed by the Royal Canadian Mint to commemorate the 200th anniversary of the discovery of the element nickel by a Swedish chemist. The concept for the landmark was developed by businessman Ted Szilva, who wanted to create a "numismatic park" that featured coin replicas and themed attractions for children.

Year built: 1964, refurbished in 2001
Size: 9.1 m in diameter, 60 cm thick
Material: stainless steel
Location: on the grounds of the Dynamic Earth facility

Thermometer
White River, ON

Size: 7.6 m high
Material: wood
Location: at Bagdon's Esso station on Highway 17

Although best known as the hometown of Winnie the Pooh, White River also advertises itself as the "Coldest Spot in Canada" because it once recorded a temperature of –58°C. However, the coldest spot in Canada is actually Snag, Yukon, with a record low temperature of –62.8°C in 1947.

Flying Saucer
Moonbeam, ON

Moonbeam is a small francophone community of about 1100 people. It got its name from pioneers in the early 1900s who claimed to see flashing lights, which they called "moonbeams," falling from the sky. The town mascot is a little green alien named Kilo.

Year built: 1991
Size: 2.7 m high, 5.5 m across
Material: fibreglass; steel legs
Location: on Highway 11

Big Joe Mufferaw
Mattawa, ON

Year built: 2005
Size: 5.2 m
Material: wood
Location: at Explorer's Point next to the Mattawa District Museum

Big Joe Mufferaw is a French Canadian folk hero, likely based on strongman and logger Joseph Montferrand (1802–64). The Paul Bunyan-esque character made his living chopping down trees and defending oppressed French Canadian loggers against their English Canadian bosses. The statue was carved by local artist Peter Cianafrani shortly before he died.

Ms. Claybelt the Cow
Temiskaming Shores, ON

The oversize Holstein was constructed to be not just a tourist attraction, but also to acknowledge the importance of the agricultural industry in the Little Claybelt region. The statue was created by Mid-Canada Fibreglass Ltd., the same company that made the flying saucer in Moonbeam.

Year built: 1984
Size: 3.7 m high, 5.5 m long
Material: fibreglass
Location: behind the Little Claybelt Homesteaders Museum on Highway 65 East

Wiarton Willie
Wiarton, ON

Year built: 1996
Weight: 4.5 t
Material: single piece of dolomite limestone quarried on the Bruce Peninsula
Location: Bluewater Park

In Wiarton, every February 2 since 1956, an albino groundhog named Willie (there has been a succession of them) has determined whether or not there will be six more weeks of winter. To honour their furry tourist attraction, town residents commissioned a sculpture by local artist Dave Robinson. The piece is entitled *Willie Emerging.*

Trumpeter Swan
Midland, ON

Although trumpeter swans are native to Ontario, they were extirpated over 200 years ago. In 1993, thanks to the efforts of biologist Harry Lumsden and the Wye Marsh Wildlife Centre, the species was successfully reintroduced. The statue was built to commemorate the restoration of these magnificent birds to the Georgian Bay area.

Year built: 2001
Size: 6.1 m high, wingspan 7.6 m
Weight: 1225 kg
Material: stainless steel
Location: Waterfront Park

Muskoka Chair
Gravenhurst, ON

Year built: 2010
Size: 6.4 m high, nearly 5 m wide
Material: cedar planks and plywood
Location: on Muskoka Road across the street from the Home Hardware store

This is actually Gravenhurst's second giant chair and was built by Rob Clark, the owner of the local Home Hardware. The smaller original was destroyed in a tornado in August 2009.

Avro Arrow
Barry's Bay, ON

Year built: 2003
Size: 6.7 m long,
3.9 m wide
Material: fibreglass
Location: in
Zurakowski Park

Zurakowski Park was built to commemorate the Avro CF-105 Arrow and its test pilot, local resident Janusz Zurakowski (1914–2004). The model of the Arrow was designed by Morris Towns and took 2300 hours to build.

Jumbo the Elephant
St. Thomas, ON

Year built: 1985
Size: 4 m high
Weight: *Elephant:* 34 t; *Base:* 91 t
Material: steel-reinforced concrete
Location: on Talbot Street, near the west end of town

Jumbo the elephant, the Barnum and Bailey Circus' prize attraction, died when he was struck and fatally wounded by a locomotive at the Woodworth Avenue railway crossing. The life-sized statue was built to commemorate the 100th anniversary of the pachyderm's death.

Benjo the Frog
Québec City, QC

Year built: 2004
Material: bronze
Location: in front of the Benjo toy store at 550 Boulevard Charest Est

Smiling, banjo-playing Benjo is the mascot of the toy store of the same name. The sculpture was created by artist Stephanie Marcon and is a popular photo-op for tourists of all ages.

Mount Royal Cross
Montréal, QC

Year built: 1924, refurbished in 2008
Size: 31.4 m high, 11 m across
Weight: 23.5 t
Material: 1830 pieces of steel joined by 6000 rivets
Location: northeastern summit of Mount Royal

The summit of Mount Royal has featured a cross since 1643, when Paul Chomedey de Maisonneuve erected the first one to thank the Virgin Mary for saving the city from floods. When the cross was refurbished in 2008, polychromatic LED lights were installed. Although the cross is typically lit in white, the LEDs allow it to be illuminated in any colour. It is visible from 80 kilometres away.

Lectra Haul
Asbestos, QC

Until 2012, the town of Asbestos was the site of the world's largest asbestos mine, the Jeffrey Mine. The mammoth Lectra Haul M200 was one of four purchased by the mine in early 1970 for $1.3 million each. It was first double axle, 200-tonne-capacity truck.

Year built: put on display in 1987
Size: 6.4 m high, 13.2 m long, 7.3 m wide
Weight: 227 t
Material: steel
Location: at the junction of Highway 255 (Boulevard Coakley) and Boulevard St. Luc

Restigouche Sam, the Atlantic Salmon
Campbellton, NB

Year built: 1982–83
Size: 8.5 m tall
Weight: 900 kg
Material: stainless steel
Location: on Salmon Boulevard at Andrew Street

Anglers from around the world come to Campbellton, on the banks of the Restigouche River, to fish for Atlantic salmon. To honour the game fish, the town erected a huge, stainless steel salmon sculpture on the waterfront. The statue is designed to withstand winds of more than 160 kilometres per hour.

World's Largest Maple Leaf
Millville, NB

The province of New Brunswick is well known for the spectacular fall colours of its abundant maple trees. To celebrate the millennium, the village of Millville built the a "World's Largest Maple Leaf," allowing visitors to see a beautiful autumn leaf any time of the year.

Year built: 1999
Size: 3 m high, 2.4 m wide, 10 cm thick
Material: structural steel plate
Location: on Route 104 at Howland Ridge Road

World's Largest Silver Fox
Salisbury, NB

Location: in front of the Irving Big Stop on the TransCanada

Before the rise of the animal rights movement, Salisbury was known as the "Home of the Silver Fox" and was a centre for silver fox ranching. Now that clothing made from animal fur is no longer socially acceptable, nearly all the ranches have disappeared. The statue was created as a tribute to the once-popular industry.

World's Largest Axe
Nackawic, NB

The town of Nackawic built the giant axe to celebrate being named the "Forestry Capital of Canada" in 1991. The concrete stump doubles as a stage for community events, and there is a time capsule in the head of the axe.

Year built: 1991
Size: *Axe:* 15 m tall, 7 m wide; *Stump:* 10 m in diameter
Weight: 50 t
Material: *Axe:* stainless steel; *Stump:* concrete
Location: on the waterfront

World's Largest Lobster
Shediac, NB

Year built: c1990
Size: *Lobster:* 10.7 m long, 4.9 m high, 5 m wide; *Fisherman:* 1.8 m tall
Weight: 82 t
Material: concrete and steel
Location: in Rotary Park at the western entrance to the town

The Shediac Rotary Club commissioned the lobster statue to celebrate the town's claim to fame as the "Lobster Capital of the World." Every year, the giant crustacean welcomes about 500,000 visitors to the town, many of whom come to attend the Shediac Lobster Festival.

World's Largest Semipalmated Sandpiper
Dorchester, NB

Year built: c2001
Material: carved from a single log
Location: on Main Street in front of the town hall

Every year, from mid-July to mid-September, semipalmated sandpipers migrate through the Bay of Fundy area on their way from the Arctic to South America. Over a quarter of a million of these shorebirds, 80 percent of the world's population, make their only stopover at the nearby Johnson's Mills Shorebird Reserve to rest and fuel up.

Big Wave
Halifax, NS

Year built: 1988, refurbished in 2012
Size: 3.6 m high, 9 m in diameter
Material: ferro-cement
Location: on the waterfront at Sackville Landing

The Wave, created by sculptor Donna Hiebert, was commissioned by the Halifax Waterfront Development Corporation. Despite a sign discouraging people from climbing the statue, visitors and locals alike use it as a playground of sorts. Capitulating to the inevitable, the city covered the sculpture with a rubberized coating and put a layer of playground rubber around it in 2012.

Big Fiddle
Sydney, NS

Year built: 2005
Size: 18 m tall
Weight: 9 t
Material: steel
Location: Joan
Harriss Cruise
Pavilion building
along the Esplanade

The showpiece of Sydney's waterfront, the "Largest Ceilidh Fiddle in the World," was created to celebrate the province's Celtic heritage and the many folk musicians that call Nova Scotia home. It was designed and constructed by local artist Cyril Hearn.

Blueberry
Oxford, NS

Year built: moved to Oxford in 1999
Size: 2.4 m high, 3.3 m wide (including arms)
Weight: 7.2 t
Material: steel rebar and cement
Location: in front of the Irving Mainway gas station on the Trans-Canada Highway

Oxford is the self-proclaimed "Wild Blueberry Capital of the World." The giant blueberry was originally created by the Mann family in Peticodiac, New Brunswick, as advertising for their family business. Irving Oil bought the monument and moved it to its present location in 1999.

Mastodon
Stewiacke, NS

Year built: 1995
Size: 4.5 m high, 7.5 m long, tusks 1.8 m long
Weight: 1.4 t
Material: fibreglass on a stainless steel framework
Location: at the Mastodon Ridge tourist attraction

Stewiacke's mastodon was built to commemorate the finding of a juvenile male mastodon skeleton at the National Gypsum Quarry near Milford in 1991. The statue's anatomy is based on that of a real mastodon, but the size and shape of the ears had to be guessed at.

Glooscap
Parrsborro, NS

Year built: c1972
Size: 6 m tall
Material: fibreglass
Location: west side of Town Hall

Glooscap, according to Mi'kmaq legend, was the first human, who sprang to life when a bolt of lightning hit the sand near Cape Blomidon in the Annapolis Valley. He created the Mi'kmaq people from seven sparks of his sacred fire and is said to have shaped much of the landscape of the area. The name Glooscap, from the Abenaki word *Kluscap*, means "man from nothing."

Bluefin Tuna
Charlottetown, PEI

Created by local artist Gerald Beaulieu, *Bluefin Bullet,* a life-sized sculpture of a bluefin tuna, was commissioned as part of Charlottetown's "Art in the City" project. The metal sculpture is covered with scales made of stainless steel spoons. It was intended to be the "ultimate fish lure," a commentary on public art as a means of "luring" tourists to the city.

Year built: 2011
Material: stainless steel
Location: 97 Queen Street

85

Potato
O'Leary, PEI

Year built: 1993
Size: 4.3 m high, 2.1 m in diameter
Material: fibreglass
Location: in front of the Canadian Potato Museum

The town of O'Leary is located in the heart of western PEI's potato farming region. The giant spud—a Russet Burbank—was built to commemorate the local potato industry. It stands in front of Canada's only potato museum.

Morris the Moose
Goobies, NL

Morris the Moose is a tourist attraction, as well as a reminder to drivers to be on the lookout for these massive mammals on the region's roads. The name "Morris" was chosen in a contest among all the elementary schools in the area.

Year built: 1994
Size: 3.5 m high, 3 m long
Weight: 9 t
Material: concrete, metal and rebar
Location: in front of the Irving Big Stop gas station at the intersection of the Trans-Canada and Highway 210

Giant Squid
Glovers Harbour, NL

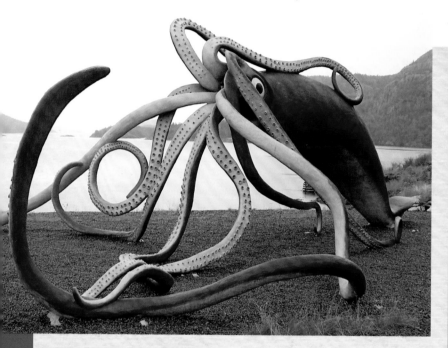

Year built: 2001
Size: 16.8 m long
Material: steel-reinforced concrete
Location: on the main road through the town

The sensational cephalopod is a life-sized replica of a giant squid that washed ashore at Thimble Tickle Bay, near the remote hamlet of Glovers Harbour, in November 1878. The super-sized squid has been certified by Guinness World Records as the "World's Largest Invertebrate."

Joey's Lookout
Gambo, NL

The town of Gambo in northeastern Newfoundland is best known as the home of Joey Smallwood, the former premier of the province and the man responsible for bringing Newfoundland into Confederation in 1949. Although the official name of the spot is Joey's Lookout, islanders reportedly call it the "Big Giant Head."

Year built: 1995
Location: next to the Trans-Canada Highway

Village Monument
Haines Junction, YT

Year built: 1987
Size: 7.3 m high
Location: in the Village Square

Haines Junction, where the Alaska Highway meets the Haines Highway at Historic Milepost 1016, is a centre for tourism because of its proximity to Kluane National Park and Reserve. The Village Monument, which features a hiker and replicas of the area's wildlife, is locally known as "the Muffin."

Signpost Forest
Watson Lake, YT

In 1942, while working on the construction of the Alcan (now the Alaska) Highway, Private Carl Lindley of Company D, 341st Army Corps of Engineers, was injured and taken to the Army Aid Station in Watson Lake. While there, he was asked to repair a directional signpost that had been damaged, and Lindley added a sign pointing toward his hometown. It read "Danville, Illinois, 2835 miles." Other travellers added signposts pointing to their hometowns, and the idea snowballed.

Year built: started in 1942
Size: nearly 100,000 signs
Location: Mile 635 on the Alaska Highway

World's Largest Gold Pan
Burwash Landing, YT

Size: 8.2 m high, 6.4 m wide
Location: next to the Kluane Museum of Natural History

This small community is located at Historic Milepost 1093 on the Alaska Highway. It became a trading post during the Kluane Gold Rush in the early 1900s. The centre of the pan features an image of a prospector panning for gold painted by Fred O'Brien, a Roman Catholic missionary.

Inukshuk
Hay River, NT

The inukshuk is a traditional Inuit construction, and its use dates back many thousands of years. It can be a navigational aid used to mark a route or a place where fish can be found, or it can serve as a memorial or indicate a place of respect. The Hay River inukshuk was built in to commemorate the Arctic Winter Games.

Year built: 1978
Size: 3 m tall
Material: stone
Location: Woodland Drive

Igloo Church
Inuvik, NT

Year built: 1960, rebuilt in 2005 after a fire
Size: *Building:* 23 m across; *Cross:* 2.7 m high, 20 m above the ground; *Cupola:* 6 m across
Location: on the corner of Loucheux Road and Breynant Street

Our Lady of Victory Church, also known as the "Igloo Church," was designed by Brother Maurice Larocque, a local Catholic missionary. Wood for the building had to be transported 1400 kilometres, and the church had to be built in such a way that the underlying permafrost would not get warm and melt, which would damage the structure.

Inukshuk
Rankin Inlet, NU

The area around Rankin Inlet has been home to the Inuit people for many centuries. The community's inukshuk was designed by Joe Nattar and built by a group of Inuit. It was created to honour the Inuit culture of the region.

Year built: 1991
Size: 4.5 m tall
Material: stone
Location: overlooking the downtown

The Publisher: Blue Bike Books
Website: www.bluebikebooks.com

Library and Archives Canada Cataloguing in Publication
Carrière, Nicholle, 1961–, author
    Weird monuments of Canada : quirky and ridiculously oversized roadside attractions / Nicholle Carrière.
    ISBN 978-1-926700-63-2 (pbk.)
        1. Monuments—Canada—Guidebooks. 2. Roadside architecture—Canada—Guidebooks. 3. Curiosities and wonders—Canada—Guidebooks. 4. Canada—Guidebooks. I. Title.
    FC38.C373 2015   917.104'73   C2015-900206-0

Front cover: Dennis Jarvis/Flickr (main image), Stockbyte/Thinkstock (sky)
Back cover: waferboard/Flickr (Tin Soldier), Falashad/Flickr (USS *Enterprise*), Bluejaywpg/Wikipedia (Chuck the Channel Cat), fw42/Flickr (Big Nickel), BStirling/Flickr (Giant Squid), stevendpclark/Flickr (Benjo the Frog), Electronker/Flickr (Inukshuk), Max Lindenthaler/Thinkstock (Igloo Church), Smudge 9000/Flickr (Big Fiddle), jamessnazell/Thinkstock (background texture)
Photo credits: Battlefords Chamber Commerce, 35; Faye Boer, 21; Glenboro Community Development Corporation, 45; Glenn Cameron, Canadian Badlands, 27; Jean-nicholas Nault/Thinkstock, 72; Jeff Mills, 75; Jody Vanderzwaag, 46; Max Lindenthaler/Thinkstock, 94; Murphy Shewchuk/Thinkstock, 18; Town of Arborg, 47; Town of Gambo, 89; Town of Hay River, 93; Town of Kelvington, 36; Twyla Salmond, 33; Village of Paradise Hill, 37. *From Flickr:* Alan Levine, 25; Antony Stanley, 28; Brian, 80; BStirling, 88; Chilanga Cement, 86; Chris M Morris, 79; chrislstubbs, 24; Dan, 91; DavidR, 55; Dennis Jarvis, 78, 84; Doug Kerr, 85; Electronker, 95; Eli Duke, 19; Emma Jane Hogbin Westby, 66; Falashad, 30; fw42, 61; Gordon Bell, 52; grampymoose, 14; Guilhem Vellut, 8; Heather Harvey, 9; Herb Neufeld, 17; James Brooks, 92; Jen's Art and Soul, 57; Joanna Poe, 87; Jon Ross, 15; JSmith, 31, 34, 62, 70; KarenHarold, 82; Kevin M. Klerks, 32; Loozrboy, 54; Matt Boulton, 40; Morgan, 83; P199, 59, 63, 64, 69; Patty Ho, 68; Paul Jerry, 42; Peter Vanderheyden, 60; purecanucks, 43; Richie Diesterheft, 56; runran, 23, 29; Ryan Schreiber, 90; Shelly Cooke, 32; Smudge 9000, 4, 81; stevendpclark, 71; Tony Hisgett, 11; turbulentflow, 6; waferboard, 7; Wilson Hui, 20. *From Wikipedia:* Bluejaywpg, 51; Bobak Ha'Eri, 53; Brenden Van Stolk, 10; Bryan C. Passifiume, 26; Cjp24, 73; Dabbler, 5, 67; Drm310, 38, 39; Gzhao, 74; Hamedog, 16; Hohum, 77; J Hazard, 50; John Kaminski, 48; Magickallwiz, 48; Mhalifu, 22; Owen Lloyd, 12; P James Franks, 65; Rangeley, 76; Tidor Costache, 58; Trevor MacInnis, 13; Martin Oravec, 44; Wtshymanski, 49. *Illustration credits:* Graham Johnson, 24, 27, 28, 55; Roger Garcia, 7, 10, 25, 64, 68, 69

We acknowledge the financial support of the Government of Canada through the Canada Book Fund (CBF) for our publishing activities.

Canadian	Patrimoine
Heritage	canadien

Produced with the assistance of the Government of Alberta, Alberta Media Fund.

Alberta
Government